This Monthly Planner

From AUGUST 2019- JULY 2022

Belongs To:

_____

_____

_____

2019

Mon	Tue	Wed	Thu
			1
5	6	7	8
12	13	14	15
19	20	21	22
26	27	28	29

August

Fri	Sat	Sun	Goals
2	3	4	
9	10	11	
16	17	18	
23	24	25	Notes
30	31		

Week of:

Schedule

Monday
Tuesday
Wednesday
Thursday
Friday
Saturday
Sunday

Week of:

Schedule

Monday
Tuesday
Wednesday
Thursday
Friday
Saturday
Sunday

Week of:

Schedule

Monday
Tuesday
Wednesday
Thursday
Friday
Saturday
Sunday

Week of:

Schedule

- Monday
- Tuesday
- Wednesday
- Thursday
- Friday
- Saturday
- Sunday

Week of:

Schedule

- Monday
- Tuesday
- Wednesday
- Thursday
- Friday
- Saturday
- Sunday

Notes

2019

Mon	Tue	Wed	Thu
2	3	4	5
9	10	11	12
16	17	18	19
23	24	25	26
30			

September

Fri	Sat	Sun	Goals
		1	
6	7	8	
13	14	15	
20	21	22	**Notes**
27	28	29	

Week of:

Schedule

| Monday |
| Tuesday |
| Wednesday |
| Thursday |
| Friday |
| Saturday |
| Sunday |

Week of:

Schedule

| Monday |
| Tuesday |
| Wednesday |
| Thursday |
| Friday |
| Saturday |
| Sunday |

Week of:

Schedule

| Monday |
| Tuesday |
| Wednesday |
| Thursday |
| Friday |
| Saturday |
| Sunday |

Week of:

Schedule

Monday
Tuesday
Wednesday
Thursday
Friday
Saturday
Sunday

Week of:

Schedule

Monday
Tuesday
Wednesday
Thursday
Friday
Saturday
Sunday

Notes

2019

Mon	Tue	Wed	Thu
	1	2	3
7	8	9	10
14	15	16	17
21	22	23	24
28	29	30	31

October

Fri	Sat	Sun	Goals
4	5	6	
11	12	13	
18	19	20	
25	26	27	**Notes**

Week of:	Week of:	Week of:
Schedule	Schedule	Schedule
Monday	Monday	Monday
Tuesday	Tuesday	Tuesday
Wednesday	Wednesday	Wednesday
Thursday	Thursday	Thursday
Friday	Friday	Friday
Saturday	Saturday	Saturday
Sunday	Sunday	Sunday

Week of:

Schedule

Monday
Tuesday
Wednesday
Thursday
Friday
Saturday
Sunday

Week of:

Schedule

Monday
Tuesday
Wednesday
Thursday
Friday
Saturday
Sunday

Notes

2019

Mon	Tue	Wed	Thu
4	5	6	7
11	12	13	14
18	19	20	21
25	26	27	28

November

Fri	Sat	Sun	Goals
1	2	3	
8	9	10	
15	16	17	
22	23	24	**Notes**
29	30		

Week of: _____

Schedule

Monday
Tuesday
Wednesday
Thursday
Friday
Saturday
Sunday

Week of: _____

Schedule

Monday
Tuesday
Wednesday
Thursday
Friday
Saturday
Sunday

Week of: _____

Schedule

Monday
Tuesday
Wednesday
Thursday
Friday
Saturday
Sunday

Week of:

Schedule

Monday
Tuesday
Wednesday
Thursday
Friday
Saturday
Sunday

Week of:

Schedule

Monday
Tuesday
Wednesday
Thursday
Friday
Saturday
Sunday

Notes

2019

Mon	Tue	Wed	Thu
2	3	4	5
9	10	11	12
16	17	18	19
23	24	25	26
30	31		

December

Fri	Sat	Sun	Goals
		1	
6	7	8	
13	14	15	
20	21	22	**Notes**
27	28	29	

Week of:

Schedule

Monday
Tuesday
Wednesday
Thursday
Friday
Saturday
Sunday

Week of:

Schedule

Monday
Tuesday
Wednesday
Thursday
Friday
Saturday
Sunday

Week of:

Schedule

Monday
Tuesday
Wednesday
Thursday
Friday
Saturday
Sunday

Week of:

Schedule

Monday
Tuesday
Wednesday
Thursday
Friday
Saturday
Sunday

Week of:

Schedule

Monday
Tuesday
Wednesday
Thursday
Friday
Saturday
Sunday

Notes

2020

Mon	Tue	Wed	Thu
		1	2
6	7	8	9
13	14	15	16
20	21	22	23
27	28	29	30

January

Fri	Sat	Sun	Goals
3	4	5	
10	11	12	
17	18	19	
24	25	26	**Notes**
31			

Week of:

Schedule

- Monday
- Tuesday
- Wednesday
- Thursday
- Friday
- Saturday
- Sunday

Week of:

Schedule

- Monday
- Tuesday
- Wednesday
- Thursday
- Friday
- Saturday
- Sunday

Week of:

Schedule

- Monday
- Tuesday
- Wednesday
- Thursday
- Friday
- Saturday
- Sunday

Week of:

Schedule

Monday
Tuesday
Wednesday
Thursday
Friday
Saturday
Sunday

Week of:

Schedule

Monday
Tuesday
Wednesday
Thursday
Friday
Saturday
Sunday

Notes

2020

Mon	Tue	Wed	Thu
3	4	5	6
10	11	12	13
17	18	19	20
24	25	26	27

February

Fri	Sat	Sun	Goals
	1	2	
7	8	9	
14	15	16	
21	22	23	**Notes**
28	29		

Week of:	Week of:	Week of:
Schedule	Schedule	Schedule
Monday	Monday	Monday
Tuesday	Tuesday	Tuesday
Wednesday	Wednesday	Wednesday
Thursday	Thursday	Thursday
Friday	Friday	Friday
Saturday	Saturday	Saturday
Sunday	Sunday	Sunday

Week of:

Schedule

| Monday |
| Tuesday |
| Wednesday |
| Thursday |
| Friday |
| Saturday |
| Sunday |

Week of:

Schedule

| Monday |
| Tuesday |
| Wednesday |
| Thursday |
| Friday |
| Saturday |
| Sunday |

Notes

2020

Mon	Tue	Wed	Thu
2	3	4	5
9	10	11	12
16	17	18	19
23	24	25	26
30	31		

March

Fri	Sat	Sun	Goals
		1	
6	7	8	
13	14	15	
20	21	22	**Notes**
27	28	29	

Week of:

Schedule

Monday
Tuesday
Wednesday
Thursday
Friday
Saturday
Sunday

Week of:

Schedule

Monday
Tuesday
Wednesday
Thursday
Friday
Saturday
Sunday

Week of:

Schedule

Monday
Tuesday
Wednesday
Thursday
Friday
Saturday
Sunday

Week of:

Schedule

- Monday
- Tuesday
- Wednesday
- Thursday
- Friday
- Saturday
- Sunday

Week of:

Schedule

- Monday
- Tuesday
- Wednesday
- Thursday
- Friday
- Saturday
- Sunday

Notes

2020

Mon	Tue	Wed	Thu
		1	2
6	7	8	9
13	14	15	16
20	21	22	23
27	28	29	30

April

Fri	Sat	Sun	Goals
3	4	5	---------------- ---------------- ---------------- ---------------- ----------------
10	11	12	---------------- ---------------- ---------------- ---------------- ----------------
17	18	19	---------------- ---------------- ---------------- ----------------
24	25	26	**Notes** ---------------- ---------------- ----------------
			---------------- ---------------- ---------------- ----------------

Week of:

Schedule

Monday
Tuesday
Wednesday
Thursday
Friday
Saturday
Sunday

Week of:

Schedule

Monday
Tuesday
Wednesday
Thursday
Friday
Saturday
Sunday

Week of:

Schedule

Monday
Tuesday
Wednesday
Thursday
Friday
Saturday
Sunday

Week of:

Schedule

Monday
Tuesday
Wednesday
Thursday
Friday
Saturday
Sunday

Week of:

Schedule

Monday
Tuesday
Wednesday
Thursday
Friday
Saturday
Sunday

Notes

2020

Mon	Tue	Wed	Thu
4	5	6	7
11	12	13	14
18	19	20	21
25	26	27	28

May

Fri	Sat	Sun	Goals
1	2	3	
8	9	10	
15	16	17	
22	23	24	Notes
29	30	31	

Week of:

Schedule

Monday
Tuesday
Wednesday
Thursday
Friday
Saturday
Sunday

Week of:

Schedule

Monday
Tuesday
Wednesday
Thursday
Friday
Saturday
Sunday

Week of:

Schedule

Monday
Tuesday
Wednesday
Thursday
Friday
Saturday
Sunday

Week of:

Schedule

Monday
Tuesday
Wednesday
Thursday
Friday
Saturday
Sunday

Week of:

Schedule

Monday
Tuesday
Wednesday
Thursday
Friday
Saturday
Sunday

Notes

2020

Mon	Tue	Wed	Thu
1	2	3	4
8	9	10	11
15	16	17	18
22	23	24	25
29	30		

June

Fri	Sat	Sun	Goals
5	6	7	
12	13	14	
19	20	21	
26	27	28	**Notes**

Week of:

Schedule

| Monday |
| Tuesday |
| Wednesday |
| Thursday |
| Friday |
| Saturday |
| Sunday |

Week of:

Schedule

| Monday |
| Tuesday |
| Wednesday |
| Thursday |
| Friday |
| Saturday |
| Sunday |

Week of:

Schedule

| Monday |
| Tuesday |
| Wednesday |
| Thursday |
| Friday |
| Saturday |
| Sunday |

Week of:

Schedule

Monday
Tuesday
Wednesday
Thursday
Friday
Saturday
Sunday

Week of:

Schedule

Monday
Tuesday
Wednesday
Thursday
Friday
Saturday
Sunday

Notes

2020

	Mon	Tue	Wed	Thu
			1	2
	6	7	8	9
	13	14	15	16
	20	21	22	23
	27	28	29	30

July

Fri	Sat	Sun	Goals
3	4	5	
10	11	12	
17	18	19	
24	25	26	**Notes**
31			

Week of:

Schedule

| Monday |
| Tuesday |
| Wednesday |
| Thursday |
| Friday |
| Saturday |
| Sunday |

Week of:

Schedule

| Monday |
| Tuesday |
| Wednesday |
| Thursday |
| Friday |
| Saturday |
| Sunday |

Week of:

Schedule

| Monday |
| Tuesday |
| Wednesday |
| Thursday |
| Friday |
| Saturday |
| Sunday |

Week of:

Schedule

- Monday
- Tuesday
- Wednesday
- Thursday
- Friday
- Saturday
- Sunday

Week of:

Schedule

- Monday
- Tuesday
- Wednesday
- Thursday
- Friday
- Saturday
- Sunday

Notes

2020

Mon	Tue	Wed	Thu
3	4	5	6
10	11	12	13
17	18	19	20
24 / 31	25	26	27

August

Fri	Sat	Sun	Goals
	1	2	
7	8	9	
14	15	16	
21	22	23	**Notes**
28	29	30	

Week of:

Schedule

Monday
Tuesday
Wednesday
Thursday
Friday
Saturday
Sunday

Week of:

Schedule

Monday
Tuesday
Wednesday
Thursday
Friday
Saturday
Sunday

Week of:

Schedule

Monday
Tuesday
Wednesday
Thursday
Friday
Saturday
Sunday

Week of:

Schedule

Monday
Tuesday
Wednesday
Thursday
Friday
Saturday
Sunday

Week of:

Schedule

Monday
Tuesday
Wednesday
Thursday
Friday
Saturday
Sunday

Notes

2020

Mon	Tue	Wed	Thu
	1	2	3
7	8	9	10
14	15	16	17
21	22	23	24
28	29	30	

September

Fri	Sat	Sun	Goals
4	5	6	
11	12	13	
18	19	20	
25	26	27	Notes

Week of:

Schedule

Monday
Tuesday
Wednesday
Thursday
Friday
Saturday
Sunday

Week of:

Schedule

Monday
Tuesday
Wednesday
Thursday
Friday
Saturday
Sunday

Week of:

Schedule

Monday
Tuesday
Wednesday
Thursday
Friday
Saturday
Sunday

// Week of:

Schedule

Monday

Tuesday

Wednesday

Thursday

Friday

Saturday

Sunday

// Week of:

Schedule

Monday

Tuesday

Wednesday

Thursday

Friday

Saturday

Sunday

Notes

2020

Mon	Tue	Wed	Thu
			1
5	6	7	8
12	13	14	15
19	20	21	22
26	27	28	29

October

Fri	Sat	Sun	Goals
2	3	4	
9	10	11	
16	17	18	
23	24	25	Notes
30	31		

Week of:

Schedule

- Monday
- Tuesday
- Wednesday
- Thursday
- Friday
- Saturday
- Sunday

Week of:

Schedule

- Monday
- Tuesday
- Wednesday
- Thursday
- Friday
- Saturday
- Sunday

Week of:

Schedule

- Monday
- Tuesday
- Wednesday
- Thursday
- Friday
- Saturday
- Sunday

Week of:

Schedule

Monday
Tuesday
Wednesday
Thursday
Friday
Saturday
Sunday

Week of:

Schedule

Monday
Tuesday
Wednesday
Thursday
Friday
Saturday
Sunday

Notes

2020

Mon	Tue	Wed	Thu
2	3	4	5
9	10	11	12
16	17	18	19
23 / 30	24	25	26

November

Fri	Sat	Sun	Goals
		1	
6	7	8	
13	14	15	
20	21	22	**Notes**
27	28	29	

Week of:

Schedule

| Monday |
| Tuesday |
| Wednesday |
| Thursday |
| Friday |
| Saturday |
| Sunday |

Week of:

Schedule

| Monday |
| Tuesday |
| Wednesday |
| Thursday |
| Friday |
| Saturday |
| Sunday |

Week of:

Schedule

| Monday |
| Tuesday |
| Wednesday |
| Thursday |
| Friday |
| Saturday |
| Sunday |

Week of:

Schedule

Monday

Tuesday

Wednesday

Thursday

Friday

Saturday

Sunday

Week of:

Schedule

Monday

Tuesday

Wednesday

Thursday

Friday

Saturday

Sunday

Notes

2020

Mon	Tue	Wed	Thu
	1	2	3
7	8	9	10
14	15	16	17
21	22	23	24
28	29	30	31

December

Fri	Sat	Sun	Goals
4	5	6	
11	12	13	
18	19	20	
25	26	27	**Notes**

Week of:

Schedule

- Monday
- Tuesday
- Wednesday
- Thursday
- Friday
- Saturday
- Sunday

Week of:

Schedule

- Monday
- Tuesday
- Wednesday
- Thursday
- Friday
- Saturday
- Sunday

Week of:

Schedule

- Monday
- Tuesday
- Wednesday
- Thursday
- Friday
- Saturday
- Sunday

Week of:

Schedule

- Monday
- Tuesday
- Wednesday
- Thursday
- Friday
- Saturday
- Sunday

Week of:

Schedule

- Monday
- Tuesday
- Wednesday
- Thursday
- Friday
- Saturday
- Sunday

Notes

2021

Mon	Tue	Wed	Thu
4	5	6	7
11	12	13	14
18	19	20	21
25	26	27	28

January

Fri	Sat	Sun	Goals
1	2	3	
8	9	10	
15	16	17	
22	23	24	**Notes**
29	30	31	

Week of:

Schedule

Monday
Tuesday
Wednesday
Thursday
Friday
Saturday
Sunday

Week of:

Schedule

Monday
Tuesday
Wednesday
Thursday
Friday
Saturday
Sunday

Week of:

Schedule

Monday
Tuesday
Wednesday
Thursday
Friday
Saturday
Sunday

Week of:

Schedule

- Monday
- Tuesday
- Wednesday
- Thursday
- Friday
- Saturday
- Sunday

Week of:

Schedule

- Monday
- Tuesday
- Wednesday
- Thursday
- Friday
- Saturday
- Sunday

Notes

2021

Mon	Tue	Wed	Thu
1	2	3	4
8	9	10	11
15	16	17	18
22	23	24	25

February

Fri	Sat	Sun	Goals
5	6	7	....
12	13	14	....
19	20	21	....
26	27	28	**Notes**
			....

Week of: _____

Schedule

Monday

Tuesday

Wednesday

Thursday

Friday

Saturday

Sunday

Week of: _____

Schedule

Monday

Tuesday

Wednesday

Thursday

Friday

Saturday

Sunday

Week of: _____

Schedule

Monday

Tuesday

Wednesday

Thursday

Friday

Saturday

Sunday

Week of:

Schedule

Monday

Tuesday

Wednesday

Thursday

Friday

Saturday

Sunday

Week of:

Schedule

Monday

Tuesday

Wednesday

Thursday

Friday

Saturday

Sunday

Notes

2021

Mon	Tue	Wed	Thu
1	2	3	4
8	9	10	11
15	16	17	18
22	23	24	25
29	30	31	

March

Fri	Sat	Sun	Goals
5	6	7	
12	13	14	
19	20	21	
26	27	28	**Notes**

Week of:	Week of:	Week of:
Schedule	Schedule	Schedule
Monday	Monday	Monday
Tuesday	Tuesday	Tuesday
Wednesday	Wednesday	Wednesday
Thursday	Thursday	Thursday
Friday	Friday	Friday
Saturday	Saturday	Saturday
Sunday	Sunday	Sunday

Week of:

Schedule

Monday
Tuesday
Wednesday
Thursday
Friday
Saturday
Sunday

Week of:

Schedule

Monday
Tuesday
Wednesday
Thursday
Friday
Saturday
Sunday

Notes

2021

Mon	Tue	Wed	Thu
			1
5	6	7	8
12	13	14	15
19	20	21	22
26	27	28	29

April

Fri	Sat	Sun	Goals
2	3	4	
9	10	11	
16	17	18	
23	24	25	**Notes**
30			

Week of:

Schedule

Monday
Tuesday
Wednesday
Thursday
Friday
Saturday
Sunday

Week of:

Schedule

Monday
Tuesday
Wednesday
Thursday
Friday
Saturday
Sunday

Week of:

Schedule

Monday
Tuesday
Wednesday
Thursday
Friday
Saturday
Sunday

Week of:

Schedule

Monday

Tuesday

Wednesday

Thursday

Friday

Saturday

Sunday

Week of:

Schedule

Monday

Tuesday

Wednesday

Thursday

Friday

Saturday

Sunday

Notes

2021

Mon	Tue	Wed	Thu
3	4	5	6
10	11	12	13
17	18	19	20
24 / 31	25	26	27

May

Fri	Sat	Sun	Goals
	1	2	
7	8	9	
14	15	16	
21	22	23	**Notes**
28	29	30	

Week of:

Schedule

Monday
Tuesday
Wednesday
Thursday
Friday
Saturday
Sunday

Week of:

Schedule

Monday
Tuesday
Wednesday
Thursday
Friday
Saturday
Sunday

Week of:

Schedule

Monday
Tuesday
Wednesday
Thursday
Friday
Saturday
Sunday

Week of:

Schedule

Monday
Tuesday
Wednesday
Thursday
Friday
Saturday
Sunday

Week of:

Schedule

Monday
Tuesday
Wednesday
Thursday
Friday
Saturday
Sunday

Notes

2021

Mon	Tue	Wed	Thu
	1	2	3
7	8	9	10
14	15	16	17
21	22	23	24
28	29	30	

June

Fri	Sat	Sun	Goals
4	5	6	
11	12	13	
18	19	20	
25	26	27	**Notes**

Week of:

Schedule

| Monday |
| Tuesday |
| Wednesday |
| Thursday |
| Friday |
| Saturday |
| Sunday |

Week of:

Schedule

| Monday |
| Tuesday |
| Wednesday |
| Thursday |
| Friday |
| Saturday |
| Sunday |

Week of:

Schedule

| Monday |
| Tuesday |
| Wednesday |
| Thursday |
| Friday |
| Saturday |
| Sunday |

Week of:

Schedule

Monday

Tuesday

Wednesday

Thursday

Friday

Saturday

Sunday

Week of:

Schedule

Monday

Tuesday

Wednesday

Thursday

Friday

Saturday

Sunday

Notes

2021

Mon	Tue	Wed	Thu
			1
5	6	7	8
12	13	14	15
19	20	21	22
26	27	28	29

July

Fri	Sat	Sun	Goals
2	3	4	
9	10	11	
16	17	18	
23	24	25	Notes
30	31		

Week of:

Schedule

Monday
Tuesday
Wednesday
Thursday
Friday
Saturday
Sunday

Week of:

Schedule

Monday
Tuesday
Wednesday
Thursday
Friday
Saturday
Sunday

Week of:

Schedule

Monday
Tuesday
Wednesday
Thursday
Friday
Saturday
Sunday

Week of:

Schedule

Monday
Tuesday
Wednesday
Thursday
Friday
Saturday
Sunday

Week of:

Schedule

Monday
Tuesday
Wednesday
Thursday
Friday
Saturday
Sunday

Notes

2021

Mon	Tue	Wed	Thu
2	3	4	5
9	10	11	12
16	17	18	19
23	24	25	26
30	31		

August

Fri	Sat	Sun	Goals
		1	
6	7	8	
13	14	15	
20	21	22	Notes
27	28	29	

Week of:

Schedule

| Monday |
| Tuesday |
| Wednesday |
| Thursday |
| Friday |
| Saturday |
| Sunday |

Week of:

Schedule

| Monday |
| Tuesday |
| Wednesday |
| Thursday |
| Friday |
| Saturday |
| Sunday |

Week of:

Schedule

| Monday |
| Tuesday |
| Wednesday |
| Thursday |
| Friday |
| Saturday |
| Sunday |

Week of:

Schedule

- Monday
- Tuesday
- Wednesday
- Thursday
- Friday
- Saturday
- Sunday

Week of:

Schedule

- Monday
- Tuesday
- Wednesday
- Thursday
- Friday
- Saturday
- Sunday

Notes

2021

Mon	Tue	Wed	Thu
		1	2
6	7	8	9
13	14	15	16
20	21	22	23
27	28	29	30

September

Fri	Sat	Sun	Goals
3	4	5	
10	11	12	
17	18	19	
24	25	26	**Notes**

Week of:

Schedule

Monday
Tuesday
Wednesday
Thursday
Friday
Saturday
Sunday

Week of:

Schedule

Monday
Tuesday
Wednesday
Thursday
Friday
Saturday
Sunday

Week of:

Schedule

Monday
Tuesday
Wednesday
Thursday
Friday
Saturday
Sunday

Week of:

Schedule

Monday

Tuesday

Wednesday

Thursday

Friday

Saturday

Sunday

Week of:

Schedule

Monday

Tuesday

Wednesday

Thursday

Friday

Saturday

Sunday

Notes

2021

Mon	Tue	Wed	Thu
4	5	6	7
11	12	13	14
18	19	20	21
25	26	27	28

October

Fri	Sat	Sun	Goals
1	2	3	
8	9	10	
15	16	17	
22	23	24	**Notes**
29	30	31	

Week of:

Schedule

Monday
Tuesday
Wednesday
Thursday
Friday
Saturday
Sunday

Week of:

Schedule

Monday
Tuesday
Wednesday
Thursday
Friday
Saturday
Sunday

Week of:

Schedule

Monday
Tuesday
Wednesday
Thursday
Friday
Saturday
Sunday

Week of:

Schedule

- Monday
- Tuesday
- Wednesday
- Thursday
- Friday
- Saturday
- Sunday

Week of:

Schedule

- Monday
- Tuesday
- Wednesday
- Thursday
- Friday
- Saturday
- Sunday

Notes

2021

Mon	Tue	Wed	Thu
1	2	3	4
8	9	10	11
15	16	17	18
22	23	24	25
29	30		

November

Fri	Sat	Sun	Goals
5	6	7	
12	13	14	
19	20	21	
26	27	28	**Notes**

Week of:

Schedule

Monday
Tuesday
Wednesday
Thursday
Friday
Saturday
Sunday

Week of:

Schedule

Monday
Tuesday
Wednesday
Thursday
Friday
Saturday
Sunday

Week of:

Schedule

Monday
Tuesday
Wednesday
Thursday
Friday
Saturday
Sunday

Week of:

Schedule

| Monday |
| Tuesday |
| Wednesday |
| Thursday |
| Friday |
| Saturday |
| Sunday |

Week of:

Schedule

| Monday |
| Tuesday |
| Wednesday |
| Thursday |
| Friday |
| Saturday |
| Sunday |

Notes

2021

Mon	Tue	Wed	Thu
		1	2
6	7	8	9
13	14	15	16
20	21	22	23
27	28	29	30

December

Fri	Sat	Sun	Goals
3	4	5	
10	11	12	
17	18	19	
24	25	26	**Notes**
31			

Week of:

Schedule

Monday
Tuesday
Wednesday
Thursday
Friday
Saturday
Sunday

Week of:

Schedule

Monday
Tuesday
Wednesday
Thursday
Friday
Saturday
Sunday

Week of:

Schedule

Monday
Tuesday
Wednesday
Thursday
Friday
Saturday
Sunday

Week of:

Schedule

Monday
Tuesday
Wednesday
Thursday
Friday
Saturday
Sunday

Week of:

Schedule

Monday
Tuesday
Wednesday
Thursday
Friday
Saturday
Sunday

Notes

2022

Mon	Tue	Wed	Thu
3	4	5	6
10	11	12	13
17	18	19	20
24	25	26	27
31			

January

Fri	Sat	Sun	Goals
	1	2	
7	8	9	
14	15	16	
21	22	23	**Notes**
28	29	30	

Week of:

Schedule

Monday
Tuesday
Wednesday
Thursday
Friday
Saturday
Sunday

Week of:

Schedule

Monday
Tuesday
Wednesday
Thursday
Friday
Saturday
Sunday

Week of:

Schedule

Monday
Tuesday
Wednesday
Thursday
Friday
Saturday
Sunday

Week of:

Schedule

Monday

Tuesday

Wednesday

Thursday

Friday

Saturday

Sunday

Week of:

Schedule

Monday

Tuesday

Wednesday

Thursday

Friday

Saturday

Sunday

Notes

2022

Mon	Tue	Wed	Thu
	1	2	3
7	8	9	10
14	15	16	17
21	22	23	24
28			

February

Fri	Sat	Sun	Goals
4	5	6	
11	12	13	
18	19	20	
25	26	27	**Notes**

Week of:

Schedule

Monday
Tuesday
Wednesday
Thursday
Friday
Saturday
Sunday

Week of:

Schedule

Monday
Tuesday
Wednesday
Thursday
Friday
Saturday
Sunday

Week of:

Schedule

Monday
Tuesday
Wednesday
Thursday
Friday
Saturday
Sunday

Week of:

Schedule

Monday

Tuesday

Wednesday

Thursday

Friday

Saturday

Sunday

Week of:

Schedule

Monday

Tuesday

Wednesday

Thursday

Friday

Saturday

Sunday

Notes

2022

Mon	Tue	Wed	Thu
	1	2	3
7	8	9	10
14	15	16	17
21	22	23	24
28	29	30	31

March

Fri	Sat	Sun	Goals
4	5	6	
11	12	13	
18	19	20	
25	26	27	Notes

Week of:

Schedule

Monday
Tuesday
Wednesday
Thursday
Friday
Saturday
Sunday

Week of:

Schedule

Monday
Tuesday
Wednesday
Thursday
Friday
Saturday
Sunday

Week of:

Schedule

Monday
Tuesday
Wednesday
Thursday
Friday
Saturday
Sunday

Week of:

Schedule

Monday

Tuesday

Wednesday

Thursday

Friday

Saturday

Sunday

Week of:

Schedule

Monday

Tuesday

Wednesday

Thursday

Friday

Saturday

Sunday

Notes

2022

Mon	Tue	Wed	Thu
4	5	6	7
11	12	13	14
18	19	20	21
25	26	27	28

April

Fri	Sat	Sun	Goals
1	2	3	
8	9	10	
15	16	17	
22	23	24	Notes
29	30		

Week of:

Schedule

Monday
Tuesday
Wednesday
Thursday
Friday
Saturday
Sunday

Week of:

Schedule

Monday
Tuesday
Wednesday
Thursday
Friday
Saturday
Sunday

Week of:

Schedule

Monday
Tuesday
Wednesday
Thursday
Friday
Saturday
Sunday

Week of:

Schedule

Monday

Tuesday

Wednesday

Thursday

Friday

Saturday

Sunday

Week of:

Schedule

Monday

Tuesday

Wednesday

Thursday

Friday

Saturday

Sunday

Notes

2022

Mon	Tue	Wed	Thu
2	3	4	5
9	10	11	12
16	17	18	19
23	24	25	26
30	31		

May

Fri	Sat	Sun	Goals
		1	
6	7	8	
13	14	15	
20	21	22	**Notes**
27	28	29	

Week of:

Schedule

Monday
Tuesday
Wednesday
Thursday
Friday
Saturday
Sunday

Week of:

Schedule

Monday
Tuesday
Wednesday
Thursday
Friday
Saturday
Sunday

Week of:

Schedule

Monday
Tuesday
Wednesday
Thursday
Friday
Saturday
Sunday

Week of:

Schedule

Monday
Tuesday
Wednesday
Thursday
Friday
Saturday
Sunday

Week of:

Schedule

Monday
Tuesday
Wednesday
Thursday
Friday
Saturday
Sunday

Notes

2022

Mon	Tue	Wed	Thu
		1	2
6	7	8	9
13	14	15	16
20	21	22	23
27	28	29	30

June

Fri	Sat	Sun	Goals
3	4	5	
10	11	12	
17	18	19	
24	25	26	**Notes**

Week of:

Schedule

Monday
Tuesday
Wednesday
Thursday
Friday
Saturday
Sunday

Week of:

Schedule

Monday
Tuesday
Wednesday
Thursday
Friday
Saturday
Sunday

Week of:

Schedule

Monday
Tuesday
Wednesday
Thursday
Friday
Saturday
Sunday

Week of:

Schedule

Monday
Tuesday
Wednesday
Thursday
Friday
Saturday
Sunday

Week of:

Schedule

Monday
Tuesday
Wednesday
Thursday
Friday
Saturday
Sunday

Notes

2022

Mon	Tue	Wed	Thu
4	5	6	7
11	12	13	14
18	19	20	21
25	26	27	28

July

Fri	Sat	Sun	Goals
1	2	3	
8	9	10	
15	16	17	
22	23	24	Notes
29	30	31	

Week of:

Schedule

Monday
Tuesday
Wednesday
Thursday
Friday
Saturday
Sunday

Week of:

Schedule

Monday
Tuesday
Wednesday
Thursday
Friday
Saturday
Sunday

Week of:

Schedule

Monday
Tuesday
Wednesday
Thursday
Friday
Saturday
Sunday

Week of:

Schedule

Monday
Tuesday
Wednesday
Thursday
Friday
Saturday
Sunday

Week of:

Schedule

Monday
Tuesday
Wednesday
Thursday
Friday
Saturday
Sunday

Notes

Made in United States
Cleveland, OH
20 May 2025